MW00488017

Contents

Patio Parties

Corn on the Cob with Garlic Herb Butter

- 1/2 cup (1 stick) unsalted butter, softened
- 3 to 4 cloves garlic, minced
- 2 tablespoons finely minced fresh parsley
- 4 to 5 ears of corn, husked
  Salt and black pepper

1. Combine butter, garlic and parsley in small bowl.

2. Place each ear of corn on a piece of aluminum foil and generously spread with butter mixture. Season with salt and pepper and tightly seal foil. Place in **CROCK-POT**® slow cooker; overlap ears, if necessary. Add enough water to come one fourth of the way up ears. Cover; cook on LOW 4 to 5 hours or on HIGH 2 to 2½ hours.

Makes 4 to 5 servings

Confetti Black Beans

- 1 cup dried black beans
- 1 1/2 teaspoons olive oil
- 1 onion, chopped
- 1/4 cup chopped red bell pepper
- 1/4 cup chopped yellow bell pepper
- 1 jalapeño pepper, finely chopped*
- 1 tomato, seeded and chopped
- 1/2 teaspoon salt
- 1/8 teaspoon black pepper
- 2 cloves garlic, minced
- 1 can (about 14 ounces) chicken broth
- 1 bay leaf
  Hot pepper sauce (optional)

Jalapeño peppers can sting and irritate the skin, so wear rubber gloves when handling peppers and do not touch your eyes.

1. Soak beans in water in large bowl 8 hours or overnight. Drain.

2. Heat oil in large skillet over medium heat. Add onion, bell peppers and jalapeño pepper; cook and stir 5 minutes or until onion is tender. Add tomato, salt and black pepper; cook 5 minutes. Stir in garlic.

3. Place beans, broth and bay leaf in **CROCK-POT®** slow cooker. Add onion mixture to beans. Cover; cook on LOW 7 to 8 hours or on HIGH 4½ to 5 hours or until beans are tender. Remove and discard bay leaf before serving. Serve with hot pepper sauce, if desired.

Makes 6 servings

Fruit Ambrosia with Dumplings

    4 cups fresh or frozen fruit, cut into bite-size pieces*
  1/2 cup plus 2 tablespoons granulated sugar, divided
  1/2 cup warm apple or cran-apple juice
    2 tablespoons quick-cooking tapioca
    1 cup all-purpose flour
1 1/4 teaspoons baking powder
  1/4 teaspoon salt
    3 tablespoons butter or margarine, cut into small pieces
  1/2 cup milk
    1 large egg
    2 tablespoons packed light brown sugar, plus more for
      garnish

Use strawberries, raspberries or peaches.

1. Combine fruit, ½ cup granulated sugar, juice and tapioca in **CROCK-POT®** slow cooker. Cover; cook on LOW 5 to 6 hours or on HIGH 2½ to 3 hours or until thick sauce forms.

2. Combine flour, remaining 2 tablespoons granulated sugar, baking powder and salt in medium bowl. Cut in butter using pastry cutter or two knives until mixture resembles coarse crumbs. Whisk milk and egg in small bowl. Pour milk mixture into flour mixture. Stir until soft dough forms.

3. Drop dough by teaspoonfuls on top of fruit. Sprinkle with 2 tablespoons brown sugar. Cover; cook on HIGH 30 minutes to 1 hour or until toothpick inserted in dumplings comes out clean. To serve, sprinkle dumplings with additional brown sugar.

Makes 4 to 6 servings

Quinoa and Vegetable Medley

2	sweet potatoes, cut into $1/2$-inch-thick slices
1	eggplant, peeled and cut into $1/2$-inch cubes
1	tomato, cut into wedges
1	green bell pepper, sliced
1	onion, cut into wedges
$1/2$	teaspoon salt
$1/4$	teaspoon black pepper
$1/4$	teaspoon ground red pepper
1	cup uncooked quinoa
2	cups vegetable broth
2	cloves garlic, minced
$1/2$	teaspoon dried thyme
$1/4$	teaspoon dried marjoram

1. Coat **CROCK-POT®** slow cooker with nonstick cooking spray. Combine sweet potatoes, eggplant, tomato, bell pepper and onion and toss with salt, black pepper and red pepper in **CROCK-POT®** slow cooker.

2. Meanwhile, place quinoa in strainer; rinse well. Add to vegetable mixture. Stir in broth, garlic, thyme and marjoram. Cover; cook on LOW 5 hours or on HIGH 2½ hours or until quinoa is tender and broth is absorbed.

Makes 6 servings

Pear Crunch

-   1 can (8 ounces) crushed pineapple in juice, undrained
-   $1/4$ cup pineapple or apple juice
-   3 tablespoons dried cranberries
-   $1 1/2$ teaspoons quick-cooking tapioca
-   $1/4$ teaspoon vanilla
-   2 pears, cored and halved
-   $1/4$ cup granola with almonds
    Fresh mint leaves (optional)

1. Combine pineapple with juice, ¼ cup pineapple juice, cranberries, tapioca and vanilla in **CROCK-POT®** slow cooker; mix well. Place pears cut side down on pineapple mixture.

2. Cover; cook on LOW 3½ to 4½ hours. Arrange pear halves on serving bowls or plates. Spoon pineapple mixture over pear halves. Sprinkle with granola. Garnish with mint leaves.

Makes 4 servings

Spiced Apple Tea

- 3 **bags cinnamon herbal tea**
- 3 **cups boiling water**
- 2 **cups unsweetened apple juice**
- 6 **whole cloves**
- 1 **cinnamon stick**

Place tea bags in **CROCK-POT®** slow cooker. Pour boiling water over tea bags; cover and let stand 10 minutes. Remove and discard tea bags. Add apple juice, cloves and cinnamon stick to **CROCK-POT®** slow cooker. Cover; cook on LOW 2 to 3 hours. Remove and discard cloves and cinnamon stick. Serve warm in mugs.

Makes 4 servings

Patio Parties

Onion Marmalade

- 1 bottle (12 ounces) balsamic vinegar
- 1 bottle (12 ounces) white wine vinegar
- 2 tablespoons water
- 3 tablespoons cornstarch or arrowroot
- 1 1/2 cups packed dark brown sugar
- 2 teaspoons cumin seeds
- 2 teaspoons coriander seeds
- 4 large yellow onions, halved and thinly sliced

1. Cook vinegars in large saucepan over high heat until reduced to ¼ cup. Sauce will be thick and syrupy. Remove from heat. Stir water into cornstarch in small bowl until smooth. Add brown sugar, cumin and coriander seeds and cornstarch mixture to sauce; blend well.

2. Place onions in **CROCK-POT®** slow cooker. Stir in sauce; mix well. Cover; cook on LOW 8 to 10 hours or on HIGH 4 to 6 hours or until onions are no longer crunchy. Stir occasionally to prevent sticking. Store in refrigerator for up to two weeks.

Makes 5 cups

Tip: Serve as side dish or condiment with eggs, roasted vegetables and meats, or on sandwiches.

Lemon and Tangerine Glazed Carrots

    6 **cups sliced carrots**
1 1/2 **cups apple juice**
    6 **tablespoons butter**
  1/4 **cup packed brown sugar**
    2 **tablespoons grated lemon peel**
    2 **tablespoons grated tangerine peel**
  1/2 **teaspoon salt**
      Chopped fresh parsley (optional)

Combine all ingredients except parsley in **CROCK-POT®** slow cooker. Cover; cook on LOW 4 to 5 hours or on HIGH 1 to 3 hours. Garnish with chopped parsley.

Makes 10 to 12 servings

Finer Fare

Sauvignon Blanc Beef with Beets & Thyme

- 1 pound red or yellow beets, quartered
- 2 tablespoons extra virgin olive oil
- 1 beef chuck roast (about 3 pounds)
- 1 yellow onion, peeled and quartered
- 2 cloves garlic, minced
- 5 sprigs fresh thyme
- 2 whole cloves
- 1 cup each chicken broth and Sauvignon Blanc
- 2 tablespoons tomato paste

1. Add beets to **CROCK-POT®** slow cooker. Heat oil in large skillet over medium heat. Sear roast 4 to 5 minutes on each side. Add onion and garlic; cook 5 minutes. Remove to **CROCK-POT®** slow cooker. Add thyme and cloves.

2. Combine broth, wine and tomato paste in medium bowl; mix well. Pour over roast and beets. Cover; cook on LOW 8 to 10 hours.

Makes 6 servings

Finer Fare

Sausage & Swiss Chard Mushrooms

- 2 packages (6 ounces each) baby portobello mushrooms, stemmed and caps hollowed out
- 4 tablespoons extra virgin olive oil, divided
- $1/2$ teaspoon salt, divided
- $1/2$ teaspoon black pepper, divided
- $1/2$ pound bulk pork sausage
- $1/2$ onion, finely chopped
- 2 cups chopped Swiss chard
- $1/4$ teaspoon dried thyme
- 2 tablespoons dry seasoned bread crumbs
- $1 1/2$ cups chicken broth, divided
- Grated Parmesan cheese and chopped fresh parsley

1. Brush mushrooms inside and out with 3 tablespoons oil. Season with ¼ teaspoon salt and ¼ teaspoon pepper; set aside.

2. Heat remaining 1 tablespoon oil in medium skillet over medium heat. Add sausage; cook and stir until browned. Transfer to medium bowl with slotted spoon. Add onion to skillet. Cook 3 minutes or until translucent, stirring to scrape up browned bits. Stir in chard and thyme. Cook until chard is just wilted, about 1 to 2 minutes.

3. Remove skillet from heat. Add sausage, bread crumbs, 1 tablespoon broth, remaining ¼ teaspoon salt and ¼ teaspoon pepper; mix well. Divide stuffing evenly among mushrooms. Pour remaining broth into **CROCK-POT®** slow cooker. Arrange stuffed mushrooms on bottom.

4. Cover; cook on HIGH 3 hours. Remove mushrooms with slotted spoon; discard cooking liquid. Sprinkle with cheese and parsley.

Makes 6 to 8 servings

Chicken Liver Pâté

- 1 1/2 pounds chicken livers, trimmed
- 1 onion, thinly sliced
- 3 sprigs fresh thyme
- 2 cloves garlic, crushed
- 1/2 teaspoon salt, divided
- 1 tablespoon water
- 3 tablespoons cold butter, cut into 4 pieces
- 2 tablespoons whipping cream
- 2 tablespoons sherry
- 1/2 shallot, minced
- 2 tablespoons chopped fresh parsley
- 1 tablespoon sherry vinegar
- 1/8 teaspoon sugar
- Black pepper
- Melba toast or toast points

1. Place chicken livers in **CROCK-POT®** slow cooker. Add onion, thyme, garlic, ¼ teaspoon salt and water. Cover; cook on LOW 2 hours.

2. Remove thyme sprigs; discard. Pour remaining ingredients from **CROCK-POT®** slow cooker into strainer; cool. Transfer to food processor; pulse enough to coarsely chop livers. Add butter, one piece at a time, pulsing just enough each time to combine. Add whipping cream and sherry; pulse to combine. Transfer to serving bowl.

3. Stir together shallot, parsley, vinegar, sugar, remaining ¼ teaspoon salt and pepper in small bowl. Set aside 5 minutes, then spoon over pâté. Serve with Melba toast.

Makes about 2 1/2 cups

Shrimp and Pepper Bisque

- 1 bag (12 ounces) frozen bell pepper blend, thawed
- 1/2 pound frozen cauliflower florets, thawed
- 1 stalk celery, sliced
- 1 tablespoon seafood seasoning
- 1/2 teaspoon dried thyme
- 1 can (about 14 ounces) chicken broth
- 12 ounces medium raw shrimp, peeled and deveined
- 2 cups half-and-half
- 2 to 3 green onions, finely chopped

1. Combine bell pepper blend, cauliflower, celery, seafood seasoning, thyme and broth in **CROCK-POT®** slow cooker. Cover; cook on LOW 8 hours or on HIGH 4 hours.

2. Stir in shrimp. Cover; cook 15 minutes or until shrimp are pink and opaque. Process soup in batches in blender or food processor until smooth. Return to **CROCK-POT®** slow cooker. Stir in half-and-half. Ladle into bowls and sprinkle with green onions.

Makes 4 servings

Tip: For a creamier, smoother consistency, strain through several layers of damp cheesecloth.

Saffron-Scented Shrimp Paella

3 tablespoons olive oil, divided
1 1/2 cups chopped onions
4 cloves garlic, thinly sliced
  Salt
1 cup roasted red bell pepper, diced
1 cup chopped tomato
1 bay leaf
  Pinch saffron
1 cup white wine
8 cups chicken broth
4 cups rice
25 large raw shrimp, peeled and deveined (with tails on)
  White pepper

1. Heat 2 tablespoons oil in large skillet over medium heat. Add onions, garlic and salt; cook and stir 5 minutes until onions are translucent. Add bell pepper, tomato, bay leaf and saffron; cook and stir until heated through. Add wine; cook until liquid is reduced by half. Add broth. Bring to a simmer. Stir in rice. Transfer to **CROCK-POT®** slow cooker. Cover; cook on HIGH 30 minutes to 1 hour or until all liquid is absorbed.

2. Toss shrimp in remaining 1 tablespoon oil; season with salt and white pepper. Place shrimp on rice in **CROCK-POT®** slow cooker. Cover; cook 10 minutes or until shrimp are opaque. Remove bay leaf before serving.

Makes 4 to 6 servings

Ham and Sage Stuffed Cornish Hens

- 1 cup plus 3 tablespoons sliced celery, divided
- 1 cup sliced leek (white part only)
- 2 tablespoons butter, divided
- $1/4$ cup finely diced onion
- $1/4$ cup diced smoked ham or prosciutto
- 1 cup seasoned stuffing mix
- 1 cup chicken broth
- 1 tablespoon finely chopped fresh sage leaves *or* 1 teaspoon ground sage
- 4 Cornish hens (about $1^1/2$ pounds each)
  Salt and black pepper

1. Coat **CROCK-POT®** slow cooker with nonstick cooking spray. Combine 1 cup celery and leek in **CROCK-POT®** slow cooker.

2. Melt 1 tablespoon butter in large nonstick skillet over medium heat. Add remaining 3 tablespoons celery, onion and ham. Cook 5 minutes or until onion is soft, stirring frequently. Stir in stuffing mix, broth and sage. Transfer mixture to medium bowl.

3. Rinse hens and pat dry; sprinkle inside and out with salt and pepper. Gently spoon stuffing into hens. Tie hens' drumsticks together with kitchen twine.

4. Melt remaining 1 tablespoon butter in same skillet over medium-high heat. Place 2 hens, breast sides down, in skillet and cook until brown. Transfer to prepared **CROCK-POT®** slow cooker. Repeat with remaining hens. Cover; cook on LOW 5 to 6 hours or on HIGH 3 to 4 hours. Remove twine and place hens on serving platter with vegetables; spoon cooking liquid over hens.

Makes 4 servings

Braised Sea Bass with Aromatic Vegetables

    2 tablespoons butter or olive oil
    2 bulbs fennel, thinly sliced
    3 carrots, julienned
    3 leeks, cleaned and thinly sliced
      Kosher salt and black pepper
    6 sea bass fillets or other firm white fish
      (2 to 3 pounds total)

1. Melt butter in large skillet over medium-high heat. Add fennel, carrots and leeks. Cook and stir until beginning to soften and lightly brown. Season with salt and pepper.

2. Arrange half of vegetables in bottom of **CROCK-POT®** slow cooker.

3. Season fish with salt and pepper and place on vegetables in **CROCK-POT®** slow cooker. Top with remaining vegetables. Cover; cook on LOW 2 to 3 hours or on HIGH 1 to 1½ hours or until fish is opaque.

Makes 6 servings

Fennel Braised with Tomato

         2 bulbs fennel
         1 tablespoon extra virgin olive oil
         1 onion, sliced
         1 clove garlic, sliced
         4 tomatoes, chopped
    $2/3$ cup vegetable broth or water
         3 tablespoons dry white wine or vegetable broth
         1 tablespoon chopped fresh marjoram *or* 1 teaspoon
           dried marjoram
    $1/4$ teaspoon salt
    $1/4$ teaspoon black pepper

1. Trim stems and bottoms from fennel bulbs, reserving green leafy tops for garnish. Cut each bulb lengthwise into 4 wedges.

2. Heat oil in large skillet over medium heat. Add fennel, onion and garlic; cook and stir 5 minutes or until onion is soft and translucent.

3. Combine fennel mixture with remaining ingredients in **CROCK-POT®** slow cooker. Cover; cook on LOW 2 to 3 hours or on HIGH 1 to 1½ hours or until vegetables are tender, stirring occasionally. Garnish with fennel leaves.

Makes 6 servings

Happy Holidays

Ham with Fruited Bourbon Sauce

- 1 bone-in ham, butt portion (about 6 pounds)
- 3/4 cup packed dark brown sugar
- 1/2 cup *each* apple juice and raisins
- 1 teaspoon ground cinnamon
- 1/4 teaspoon red pepper flakes
- 1/3 cup dried cherries
- 1/4 cup *each* cornstarch and bourbon

1. Coat **CROCK-POT®** slow cooker with nonstick cooking spray. Add ham, cut side up. Combine brown sugar, apple juice, raisins, cinnamon and red pepper flakes in small bowl; stir well. Pour mixture evenly over ham. Cover; cook on LOW 9 to 10 hours or on HIGH 4½ to 5 hours. Add cherries 30 minutes before end of cooking time. Turn off heat.

2. Transfer ham to cutting board; let stand 15 minutes before slicing. Let cooking liquid stand 5 minutes. Skim and discard fat.

3. Turn **CROCK-POT®** slow cooker to HIGH. Whisk cornstarch and bourbon in small bowl until cornstarch is dissolved. Stir into cooking liquid. Cover; cook on HIGH 15 to 20 minutes or until thickened. Serve sauce over sliced ham.

Makes 10 to 12 servings

Corn Bread Stuffing with Sausage & Apples

    1 package (16 ounces) honey corn bread mix,
      plus ingredients to prepare mix
    2 cups cubed French bread
1 1/2 pounds mild Italian sausage, casings removed
    1 onion, finely chopped
    1 green apple, peeled, cored and diced
    2 stalks celery, finely chopped
  1/4 teaspoon *each* dried sage, rosemary and thyme
    3 cups chicken broth

1. Mix and bake corn bread according to package directions. When cool, cover with plastic wrap and set aside overnight.

2. Coat **CROCK-POT®** slow cooker with nonstick cooking spray. Preheat oven to 350°F. Cut corn bread into 1-inch cubes. Spread corn bread and French bread on baking sheet. Toast in oven about 20 minutes or until dry.

3. Meanwhile, heat medium skillet over medium heat. Add sausage; cook and stir until browned. Transfer sausage to **CROCK-POT®** slow cooker with slotted spoon.

4. Add onion, apple and celery to skillet. Cook and stir 5 minutes or until softened. Stir in sage, rosemary and thyme. Transfer mixture to **CROCK-POT®** slow cooker.

5. Add bread cubes and stir gently to combine. Pour broth over mixture. Cover; cook on HIGH 3 to 3½ hours or until liquid is absorbed. Garnish with parsley.

Makes 8 to 12 servings

Sweet Potato & Pecan Casserole

       1 can (40 ounces) sweet potatoes, drained and mashed
 $1/2$ cup apple juice
 $1/3$ cup plus 2 tablespoons butter, melted, divided
 $1/2$ teaspoon salt
 $1/2$ teaspoon ground cinnamon
 $1/4$ teaspoon black pepper
       2 eggs
 $1/3$ cup chopped pecans
 $1/3$ cup packed brown sugar
       2 tablespoons all-purpose flour

1. Combine sweet potatoes, apple juice, ⅓ cup butter, salt, cinnamon and pepper in large bowl. Beat in eggs. Place mixture in **CROCK-POT®** slow cooker.

2. Combine pecans, brown sugar, flour and remaining 2 tablespoons butter in small bowl. Spread over sweet potatoes in **CROCK-POT®** slow cooker. Cover; cook on HIGH 3 to 4 hours.

Makes 6 to 8 servings

Roast Ham with Tangy Mustard Glaze

        1 fully cooked boneless ham (about 3 pounds),
           visible fat removed
    $1/4$ cup packed dark brown sugar
        2 tablespoons lemon juice, divided
        1 tablespoon Dijon mustard
    $1/2$ teaspoon ground allspice
    $1/4$ cup granulated sugar
        2 tablespoons cornstarch

1. Place ham in **CROCK-POT®** slow cooker. Combine brown sugar, 2 teaspoons lemon juice, mustard and allspice. Spoon evenly over ham. Cover; cook on LOW 6 to 7 hours or until ham is warm throughout and sauce is well absorbed. Transfer ham to warm serving platter.

2. Pour cooking liquid from **CROCK-POT®** slow cooker into small heavy saucepan. Add remaining lemon juice, granulated sugar and cornstarch. Cook over medium-high heat until mixture boils. Reduce to medium heat. Cook and stir until sauce is thickened and glossy.

3. Carve ham into slices and spoon sauce over individual servings.

Makes 12 to 15 servings

Green Bean Casserole

- 2 packages (10 ounces each) frozen green beans, thawed
- 1 can (10^3/$_4$ ounces) condensed cream of mushroom soup, undiluted
- 1 tablespoon chopped fresh parsley
- 1 tablespoon chopped roasted red peppers
- 1 teaspoon dried sage
- 1/2 teaspoon salt
- 1/2 teaspoon black pepper
- 1/4 teaspoon ground nutmeg
- 1/2 cup toasted slivered almonds

Combine all ingredients except almonds in **CROCK-POT®** slow cooker. Cover; cook on LOW 3 to 4 hours. Sprinkle with almonds before serving.

Makes 4 to 6 servings

Pork Roast with Currant Cherry Salsa

- 1 1/2 teaspoons chili powder
- 3/4 teaspoon salt
- 1/2 teaspoon *each* garlic powder and paprika
- 1/4 teaspoon ground allspice
- 1 boneless pork loin roast (2 pounds)
- 1/2 cup water
- 1 pound bag frozen pitted dark cherries, thawed, drained and halved
- 1/4 cup currants or dark raisins
- 1 teaspoon *each* balsamic vinegar and grated orange peel
- 1/8 to 1/4 teaspoon red pepper flakes

1. Combine chili powder, salt, garlic powder, paprika and allspice in small bowl. Coat roast evenly with spice mixture.

2. Coat large skillet with nonstick cooking spray; heat over medium-high heat. Brown roast on all sides. Place in **CROCK-POT®** slow cooker. Pour water into skillet, stirring to scrape up browned bits. Pour liquid into **CROCK-POT®** slow cooker. Cover; cook on LOW 6 to 8 hours.

3. Remove roast from **CROCK-POT®** slow cooker. Tent with foil; keep warm. Strain juices from **CROCK-POT®** slow cooker; discard solids. Pour juices into small saucepan; keep warm over low heat.

4. Add cherries, currants, vinegar, orange peel and red pepper flakes to **CROCK-POT®** slow cooker. Turn **CROCK-POT®** slow cooker to HIGH. Cover; cook on HIGH 30 minutes. Slice pork and spoon warm juices over meat. Serve with salsa.

Makes 8 servings

Pumpkin Bread Pudding

- 2 cups whole milk
- $1/2$ cup plus 2 tablespoons butter, divided
- 1 cup solid-pack pumpkin
- 3 eggs
- 1 cup packed dark brown sugar, divided
- 1 tablespoon ground cinnamon
- 2 teaspoons vanilla
- $1/2$ teaspoon ground nutmeg
- $1/4$ teaspoon salt
- 16 slices cinnamon raisin bread, torn into small pieces (8 cups total)
- $1/2$ cup whipping cream

1. Coat **CROCK-POT®** slow cooker with nonstick cooking spray. Combine milk and 2 tablespoons butter in medium microwavable bowl. Microwave on HIGH 2½ to 3 minutes or until very hot.

2. Whisk pumpkin, eggs, ½ cup brown sugar, cinnamon, vanilla, nutmeg and salt in large bowl until well blended. Whisk in milk mixture until blended. Add bread cubes; toss to coat.

3. Transfer to **CROCK-POT®** slow cooker. Cover; cook on HIGH 2 hours or until knife inserted into center comes out clean. Turn off heat. Uncover; let stand 15 minutes.

4. Combine remaining ½ cup butter, ½ cup brown sugar and cream in a small saucepan. Bring to a boil over high heat, stirring frequently. Remove from heat. Spoon bread pudding into individual bowls and top with sauce.

Makes 8 servings

Harvest Ham Supper

6 carrots, cut into 2-inch pieces
3 sweet potatoes, quartered
1 to 1 1/2 pounds boneless ham
1 cup maple syrup

1. Arrange carrots and potatoes in bottom of **CROCK-POT®** slow cooker to form rack.

2. Place ham on top of vegetables. Pour syrup over ham and vegetables. Cover; cook on LOW 6 to 8 hours.

Makes 6 servings

Contents

Asian Pork Tenderloin

- 1/2 cup bottled garlic ginger sauce
- 1/4 cup sliced green onions
- 1 pork tenderloin (about 1 pound)
- 1 red onion, cut into chunks
- 1 red bell pepper, cut into 1-inch pieces
- 1 zucchini, cut into 1/4-inch slices
- 1 tablespoon olive oil

1. Place ginger sauce and green onions in large resealable food storage bag. Add pork; seal bag and turn to coat evenly. Refrigerate 30 minutes or overnight.

2. Combine red onion, bell pepper, zucchini and oil in large bowl; toss to coat. Place vegetables in **CROCK-POT®** slow cooker. Remove pork from bag and place on top of vegetables. Discard marinade. Cover; cook on LOW 6 to 7 hours or on HIGH 4 to 5 hours.

3. Remove pork to cutting board; cover loosely with foil and let stand 10 minutes before slicing. Serve pork with vegetables.

Makes 4 servings

Lemon-Mint Red Potatoes

2 pounds new red potatoes
3 tablespoons extra virgin olive oil
1 teaspoon salt
$3/4$ teaspoon Greek seasoning or dried oregano
$1/4$ teaspoon garlic powder
$1/4$ teaspoon black pepper
$1/4$ cup chopped fresh mint, divided
2 tablespoons butter
2 tablespoons lemon juice
1 teaspoon grated lemon peel

1. Coat **CROCK-POT®** slow cooker with nonstick cooking spray. Add potatoes and oil, stirring gently to coat. Sprinkle with salt, Greek seasoning, garlic powder and pepper. Cover; cook on LOW 7 hours or on HIGH 4 hours.

2. Stir in 2 tablespoons mint, butter, lemon juice and lemon peel. Stir until butter is completely melted. Cover; cook 15 minutes to allow flavors to blend. Sprinkle with remaining mint.

Makes 4 servings

Tip: It's easy to prepare these potatoes ahead of time. Simply follow the recipe and then turn off the heat. Let it stand at room temperature for up to 2 hours. You may reheat or serve the potatoes at room temperature.

Beans with Smoky Canadian Bacon

2 cans (about 14 ounces each) diced fire-roasted tomatoes

1 can (about 15 ounces) pinto beans, rinsed and drained

1 package (8 ounces) Canadian bacon, cut into $1/2$-inch cubes

$1/2$ cup Texas-style barbecue sauce*

1 onion, finely chopped

$1/2$ teaspoon salt

$1/8$ teaspoon red pepper flakes (optional)

Black pepper

Look for barbecue sauce with liquid smoke as an ingredient.

Combine all ingredients in **CROCK-POT**® slow cooker. Cover; cook on LOW 5 to 7 hours. Serve in bowls.

Makes 4 servings

Fudge and Cream Pudding Cake

    2 tablespoons unsalted butter
    1 cup all-purpose flour
  3/4 cup packed light brown sugar
    5 tablespoons unsweetened cocoa powder, divided
    2 teaspoons baking powder
  1/2 teaspoon ground cinnamon
  1/8 teaspoon salt
    1 cup light cream
    1 tablespoon vegetable oil
    1 teaspoon vanilla
  3/4 cup packed dark brown sugar
 1 3/4 cups hot water
      Whipped cream or ice cream (optional)

1. Grease 4½-quart **CROCK-POT®** slow cooker with butter. Combine flour, light brown sugar, 3 tablespoons cocoa, baking powder, cinnamon and salt in medium bowl. Add cream, oil and vanilla; stir well to combine. Pour batter into **CROCK-POT®** slow cooker.

2. Combine dark brown sugar and remaining 2 tablespoons cocoa in medium bowl. Add hot water; stir well to combine. Pour sauce over cake batter. Do not stir. Cover; cook on HIGH 2 hours.

3. Spoon onto plates. Serve with whipped cream, if desired.

Makes 8 to 10 servings

Provençal Lemon and Olive Chicken

        2 cups chopped onion
        8 skinless chicken thighs (about 2^1/$_2$ pounds)
        1 lemon, thinly sliced and seeds removed
        1 cup pitted green olives
        1 tablespoon olive brine from jar or white vinegar
        2 teaspoons herbes de Provence
        1 bay leaf
    ^{1}/$_2$ teaspoon salt
    ^{1}/$_8$ teaspoon black pepper
        1 cup chicken broth
    ^{1}/$_2$ cup minced fresh parsley

1. Place onion in **CROCK-POT®** slow cooker. Arrange chicken over onion. Place lemon slice on each thigh. Add olives, brine, herbes de Provence, bay leaf, salt and pepper. Slowly pour in broth.

2. Cover; cook on LOW 5 to 6 hours or on HIGH 3 to 3½ hours or until chicken is tender. Remove and discard bay leaf. Stir in parsley before serving.

Makes 8 servings

Note: To skin chicken easily, grasp skin with paper towel and pull away. Repeat with fresh paper towel for each piece of chicken, discarding skins and towels.

Old-Fashioned Sauerkraut

        8 slices bacon, chopped
        2 pounds sauerkraut
        1 large head cabbage *or* 2 small heads cabbage
    2 1/2 cups chopped onions
      1/4 cup (1/2 stick) butter
        2 tablespoons sugar
        1 teaspoon salt
        1 teaspoon black pepper

1. Heat large skillet over medium heat. Add bacon; cook and stir until crisp. Remove skillet from heat and set aside. (Do not drain bacon fat.)

2. Place sauerkraut, cabbage, onions, butter, sugar, salt and pepper in **CROCK-POT®** slow cooker. Pour bacon and bacon fat over sauerkraut mixture. Cover; cook on LOW 4 to 5 hours or on HIGH 1 to 3 hours.

Makes 8 to 10 servings

Note: Serve with your favorite bratwurst, knockwurst or other sausage.

Chorizo and Corn Bread Dressing

- 1/2 **pound chorizo sausage, removed from casings***
- 1 **can (about 14 ounces) chicken broth**
- 1 **can (10 3/4 ounces) condensed cream of chicken soup, undiluted**
- 1 **box (6 ounces) corn bread stuffing mix**
- 1 **cup chopped onion**
- 1 **cup diced red bell pepper**
- 1 **cup chopped celery**
- 1 **cup frozen corn**
- 3 **eggs, lightly beaten**

A highly seasoned Mexican pork sausage.

1. Coat **CROCK-POT®** slow cooker with nonstick cooking spray.

2. Brown chorizo 6 to 8 minutes in large skillet over medium-high heat, stirring to break up meat. Transfer to **CROCK-POT®** slow cooker with slotted spoon.

3. Stir broth and chicken soup into skillet. Add remaining ingredients and stir until well blended. Stir into **CROCK-POT®** slow cooker. Cover; cook on LOW 7 hours or on HIGH 3½ hours.

Makes 4 to 6 servings

Cheesy Corn and Peppers

   2 pounds frozen corn
   2 poblano chile peppers, chopped, or 1 large green
     bell pepper and 1 jalapeño pepper, seeded and finely
     chopped*
   2 tablespoons butter, cut into cubes
   1 teaspoon salt
 $1/2$ teaspoon ground cumin
 $1/4$ teaspoon black pepper
   3 ounces cream cheese, cut into cubes
   1 cup (4 ounces) shredded sharp Cheddar cheese

*Poblano and jalapeño peppers can sting and irritate the skin, so wear
rubber gloves when handling peppers and do not touch your eyes.*

1. Coat **CROCK-POT®** slow cooker with nonstick cooking spray.
Combine all ingredients except cream cheese and Cheddar cheese in
CROCK-POT® slow cooker. Cover; cook on HIGH 2 hours.

2. Stir in cheeses. Cover; cook on HIGH 15 minutes or until cheeses are
melted.

Makes 8 servings

Simple Suppers

Boneless Chicken Cacciatore

- 2 tablespoons olive oil
- 6 boneless, skinless chicken breasts, sliced in half horizontally
- 4 cups tomato-basil pasta sauce or marinara sauce
- 1 cup coarsely chopped yellow onion
- 1 cup coarsely chopped green bell pepper
- 1 can (6 ounces) sliced mushrooms
- 1/4 cup dry red wine (optional)
- 2 teaspoons minced garlic
- 2 teaspoons dried oregano, crushed
- 2 teaspoons dried thyme, crushed
- 2 teaspoons salt
- 2 teaspoons black pepper

1. Heat oil in large skillet over medium heat. Brown chicken on both sides. Drain and transfer to **CROCK-POT®** slow cooker.

2. Add remaining ingredients; stir well to combine. Cover; cook on LOW 5 to 7 hours or on HIGH 2 to 3 hours.

Makes 6 servings

Basil Chicken Merlot with Mushrooms

- 3 tablespoons extra virgin olive oil, divided
- 1 roasting chicken (about 3 pounds), skinned and cut into individual pieces
- 1 1/2 cups thickly sliced cremini mushrooms
- 1 yellow onion, diced
- 2 cloves garlic, minced
- 1 cup chicken broth
- 1 can (6 ounces) tomato paste
- 1/3 cup Merlot or other dry red wine
- 2 teaspoons sugar
- 1 teaspoon ground oregano
- 1/4 teaspoon *each* salt and black pepper
- 2 tablespoons minced fresh basil
- 3 cups cooked ziti pasta, drained

1. Heat 1½ to 2 tablespoons oil in large skillet over medium heat. Brown half of chicken on each side about 3 to 5 minutes. Remove with slotted spoon and repeat with remaining chicken. Set aside.

2. Heat remaining oil in skillet and add mushrooms, onion and garlic. Cook and stir 7 to 8 minutes or until onion is soft. Transfer to **CROCK-POT®** slow cooker. Top with chicken.

3. Combine broth, tomato paste, wine, sugar, oregano, salt and pepper in medium bowl. Pour sauce over chicken. Cover; cook on LOW 7 to 9 hours or on HIGH 3 to 4 hours.

4. Stir in basil. Place pasta in large serving bowl or on platter. Top with chicken, mushrooms and sauce.

Makes 4 to 6 servings

Wild Rice and Mushroom Casserole

        2 tablespoons olive oil
    1/2 red onion, finely diced
        1 green bell pepper, finely diced
        8 ounces mushrooms, thinly sliced
        1 can (about 14 ounces) diced tomatoes, drained
        2 cloves garlic, minced
        1 teaspoon *each* dried oregano and paprika
        2 tablespoons butter
        2 tablespoons all-purpose flour
    1 1/2 cups milk
        8 ounces pepper jack, Cheddar or Swiss cheese, shredded
          Salt and black pepper
        2 cups wild rice, cooked according to package instructions

1. Heat oil in large skillet over medium heat. Add onion, bell pepper and mushrooms. Cook and stir 5 to 6 minutes, until vegetables are soft. Add tomatoes, garlic, oregano and paprika; cook until heated through. Transfer to large bowl; let cool.

2. Melt butter in skillet over medium heat; whisk in flour. Cook and stir 4 to 5 minutes until smooth and golden. Whisk in milk. Bring to a boil. Whisk in cheese until melted; season with salt and black pepper.

3. Combine wild rice with sautéed vegetables. Fold in cheese sauce and mix gently.

4. Coat **CROCK-POT**® slow cooker with nonstick cooking spray. Pour in wild rice mixture. Cover; cook on LOW 4 to 6 hours or on HIGH 2 to 3 hours.

Makes 4 to 6 servings

Fall-Apart Pork Roast with Mole

$2/3$ cup whole almonds

$2/3$ cup raisins

3 tablespoons vegetable oil, divided

$1/2$ cup chopped onion

4 cloves garlic, chopped

$2^3/4$ pounds lean boneless pork shoulder roast

1 can (about 14 ounces) diced fire-roasted tomatoes

1 cup cubed bread, any variety

$1/2$ cup chicken broth

2 ounces Mexican chocolate, chopped

2 tablespoons canned chipotle peppers in adobo sauce, chopped

1. Heat large skillet over medium-high heat. Add almonds and toast 3 to 4 minutes, stirring frequently, until fragrant. Add raisins. Cook and stir 1 to 2 minutes or until raisins begin to plump. Place half of almond mixture in large bowl. Reserve remaining half for garnish.

2. Heat 1 tablespoon oil in same skillet. Add onion and garlic; cook and stir 2 minutes or until softened. Add to almond mixture; set aside. Heat remaining oil in same skillet. Add pork roast and brown on all sides, about 5 to 7 minutes. Transfer to **CROCK-POT®** slow cooker.

3. Add tomatoes with juice, bread, broth, chocolate and chipotle peppers to almond mixture. Place in blender or food processor in batches; process until smooth. Pour sauce over pork in **CROCK-POT®** slow cooker. Cover; cook on LOW 7 to 8 hours or on HIGH 3 to 4 hours. Remove pork from **CROCK-POT®** slow cooker. Whisk sauce until smooth; spoon over pork. Garnish with reserved almond mixture.

Makes 6 servings

Turkey Stroganoff

- 4 **cups sliced mushrooms**
- 2 **stalks celery, thinly sliced**
- 2 **shallots or $1/2$ onion, minced**
- 1 **cup chicken broth**
- $1/2$ **teaspoon dried thyme**
- $1/4$ **teaspoon black pepper**
- 2 **turkey tenderloins, turkey breasts or boneless, skinless chicken thighs (about 10 ounces each), cut into bite-size chunks**
- $1/2$ **cup sour cream**
- 1 **tablespoon plus 1 teaspoon all-purpose flour**
- $1/4$ **teaspoon salt**
- $1 1/3$ **cups cooked wide egg noodles**

1. Coat large skillet with nonstick cooking spray. Add mushrooms, celery and shallots; cook and stir over medium heat 5 minutes or until mushrooms and shallots are tender. Spoon into **CROCK-POT®** slow cooker. Stir in broth, thyme and pepper. Stir in turkey. Cover; cook on LOW 5 to 6 hours.

2. Combine sour cream and flour in small bowl. Spoon 2 tablespoons liquid from **CROCK-POT®** slow cooker into bowl; stir well. Stir sour cream mixture into **CROCK-POT®** slow cooker. Cover; cook 10 minutes. Stir in salt. Serve noodles topped with turkey mixture.

Makes 4 servings

Asian Beef with Broccoli

  1 1/2 **pounds boneless beef chuck steak (about 1 1/2 inches thick), sliced into thin strips***

    1 **can (10 1/2 ounces) condensed beef consommé, undiluted**

  1/2 **cup oyster sauce**

    2 **tablespoons cornstarch**

    1 **bag (16 ounces) fresh broccoli florets**

       Hot cooked rice

       Sesame seeds (optional)

*To make slicing steak easier, place in freezer for 30 minutes to firm up.

1. Place beef in **CROCK-POT®** slow cooker. Pour consommé and oyster sauce over beef. Cover; cook on HIGH 3 hours.

2. Combine cornstarch and 2 tablespoons cooking liquid in small bowl. Add to **CROCK-POT®** slow cooker. Stir well to combine. Cover; cook on HIGH 15 minutes or until thickened.

3. Poke holes in broccoli bag with fork. Microwave on HIGH 3 minutes. Empty bag into **CROCK-POT®** slow cooker. Gently toss beef and broccoli together. Serve over rice. Garnish with sesame seeds.

Makes 4 to 6 servings

Macaroni and Cheese

6 cups cooked elbow macaroni

2 tablespoons butter

4 cups evaporated milk

6 cups (24 ounces) shredded Cheddar cheese

2 teaspoons salt

1/2 teaspoon black pepper

Toss macaroni with butter in large bowl. Stir in evaporated milk, cheese, salt and pepper; place in **CROCK-POT®** slow cooker. Cover; cook on HIGH 2 to 3 hours.

Makes 6 to 8 servings

Tip: Make this mac 'n' cheese recipe more fun. Add some tasty mix-ins: diced green or red bell pepper, peas, hot dog slices, chopped tomato, browned ground beef or chopped onion. Be creative!

Family Get-Togethers

Easy Mu Shu Pork

- 1 package (14 ounces) coleslaw mix, divided
- 1 package (10 ounces) shredded carrots, divided
- 1 package (6 ounces) shiitake mushrooms, sliced
- 3 cloves garlic, minced
- 3/4 cup hoisin sauce, divided
- 3 tablespoons reduced-sodium soy sauce
- 3/4 pound pork loin roast
- 12 (6-inch) flour tortillas
- 1 bunch green onions, chopped (optional)

1. Place half each of coleslaw mix and carrots in **CROCK-POT®** slow cooker. Add mushrooms; toss to combine. Stir in garlic. Add ½ cup hoisin sauce and soy sauce; stir to combine. Place pork on top of vegetables. Cover; cook on LOW 4 to 5 hours or until pork is fork-tender.

2. Shred pork with two forks. Add remaining half each of coleslaw mix and carrots, and remaining ¼ cup hoisin sauce; stir to combine.

3. Warm tortillas according to package directions. Divide pork mixture among tortillas. Top with green onions, if desired.

Makes 6 servings

Peppered Pork Cutlets with Onion Gravy

- $1/2$ teaspoon paprika
- $1/4$ teaspoon *each* ground cumin and black pepper
- 4 boneless pork cutlets (4 ounces each), trimmed of fat
- 2 cups thinly sliced onions
- 2 tablespoons all-purpose flour, divided
- $3/4$ cup water
- $1 1/2$ teaspoons chicken bouillon granules
- 2 tablespoons fat-free (skim) milk
- $1/4$ teaspoon salt

1. Combine paprika, cumin and black pepper in small bowl; blend well. Sprinkle mixture evenly over one side of each cutlet and press down gently to adhere. Let stand 15 minutes to absorb flavors.

2. Heat large skillet over medium heat. Spray with nonstick cooking spray. Add pork, seasoned side down, and cook 3 minutes or until richly browned. Remove to **CROCK-POT®** slow cooker.

3. Coat skillet with cooking spray and heat over medium-high heat. Add onions; cook 4 minutes or until richly browned, stirring frequently. Sprinkle with 1½ tablespoons flour; toss to coat. Stir in water and bouillon; bring to a boil. Add onions and any accumulated juices to **CROCK-POT®** slow cooker; spoon some sauce over pork. Cover; cook on LOW 4 to 5 hours.

4. Place pork on serving platter and set aside. Turn **CROCK-POT®** slow cooker to HIGH. Stir milk into onion mixture, or, for thicker consistency, combine milk and remaining ½ tablespoon flour and add to onion mixture. Add salt and transfer to **CROCK-POT®** slow cooker. Cook on HIGH 10 minutes or until thickened. Spoon sauce over pork.

Makes 4 servings

Super Easy Chicken Noodle Soup

- 1 can (about 48 ounces) chicken broth
- 2 boneless, skinless chicken breasts, cut into bite-size pieces
- 4 cups water
- $^2/_3$ cup diced onion
- $^2/_3$ cup diced celery
- $^2/_3$ cup diced carrots
- $^2/_3$ cup sliced mushrooms
- $^1/_2$ cup frozen peas
- 4 chicken bouillon cubes
- 2 tablespoons butter
- 1 tablespoon dried parsley flakes
- 1 teaspoon salt
- 1 teaspoon ground cumin
- 1 teaspoon dried marjoram
- 1 teaspoon black pepper
- 2 cups cooked egg noodles

Combine all ingredients except noodles in **CROCK-POT®** slow cooker. Cover; cook on LOW 5 to 7 hours or on HIGH 3 to 4 hours. Stir in noodles 30 minutes before serving.

Makes 4 servings

Roast Chicken with Peas, Prosciutto and Cream

1 whole chicken (about 2^1/$_2$ pounds), cut up
  Salt and black pepper
5 ounces prosciutto, diced
1 white onion, finely chopped
^{1}/$_2$ cup dry white wine
1 package (10 ounces) frozen peas
^{1}/$_2$ cup whipping cream
2 tablespoons water
1^1/$_2$ tablespoons cornstarch
4 cups farfalle pasta, cooked and drained

1. Season chicken with salt and pepper. Combine chicken, prosciutto, onion and wine in **CROCK-POT®** slow cooker. Cover; cook on LOW 8 to 10 hours or on HIGH 4 to 5 hours.

2. During last 30 minutes of cooking, add peas and cream to cooking liquid.

3. Remove chicken. Remove meat from bones and set aside on a warmed platter.

4. Stir water into cornstarch in small bowl until smooth. Add to cooking liquid in **CROCK-POT®** slow cooker. Cover; cook on HIGH 10 to 15 minutes or until thickened.

5. Spoon pasta onto individual plates. Place chicken on pasta and top each portion with sauce.

Makes 6 servings

Turkey Piccata

2$\frac{1}{2}$ tablespoons all-purpose flour
$\frac{1}{4}$ teaspoon salt
$\frac{1}{4}$ teaspoon black pepper
  1 pound turkey breast, cut into short strips*
  1 tablespoon butter
  1 tablespoon olive oil
$\frac{1}{2}$ cup chicken broth
  2 teaspoons freshly squeezed lemon juice
    Grated peel of 1 lemon
  2 cups cooked rice (optional)
  2 tablespoons finely chopped fresh Italian parsley

*You may substitute turkey tenderloins; cut as directed.

1. Combine flour, salt and pepper in large resealable food storage bag. Add turkey and shake well to coat. Heat butter and oil in large skillet over medium-high heat. Add turkey in single layer; brown on all sides, about 2 minutes per side. Transfer to **CROCK-POT®** slow cooker, arranging on bottom in single layer.

2. Pour broth into skillet. Cook and stir to scrape up any browned bits. Pour into **CROCK-POT®** slow cooker. Add lemon juice and peel. Cover; cook on LOW 1 hour. Serve over rice, if desired. Sprinkle with parsley before serving.

Makes 4 servings

Tip: This recipe will also work with chicken strips. Start with boneless, skinless chicken breasts, then follow the recipe as directed.

Nana's Beef Brisket

- 1 onion, thinly sliced
- 1 beef brisket (2 to 2$^1/_2$ pounds)
- $^1/_2$ teaspoon salt
- $^1/_2$ teaspoon black pepper
- $^2/_3$ cup chili sauce, divided
- 1$^1/_2$ tablespoons packed brown sugar
- $^1/_4$ teaspoon ground cinnamon
- 2 sweet potatoes, cut into 1-inch pieces
- 1 cup (5 ounces) pitted prunes
- 2 tablespoons cold water
- 2 tablespoons cornstarch

1. Place onion in **CROCK-POT®** slow cooker. Arrange brisket over onion (tucking edges under to fit, if necessary). Sprinkle with salt and pepper; top with ⅓ cup chili sauce. Cover; cook on HIGH 3½ hours.

2. Combine remaining ⅓ cup chili sauce, brown sugar and cinnamon in large bowl. Add sweet potatoes and prunes; toss to coat. Spoon mixture over brisket. Cover; cook on HIGH 1¼ to 1½ hours or until brisket and sweet potatoes are tender.

3. Transfer brisket to cutting board; tent with foil. Transfer sweet potato mixture to serving platter with slotted spoon. Keep warm.

4. Stir water into cornstarch in small bowl until smooth. Stir mixture into cooking liquid. Cover; cook on HIGH 10 minutes or until sauce is thickened.

5. Cut brisket crosswise into thin slices. Serve with sweet potato mixture and sauce.

Makes 8 servings

Pizza Soup

- 2 cans (about 14 ounces each) stewed tomatoes with Italian seasonings, undrained
- 2 cups beef broth
- 1 cup sliced mushrooms
- 1 onion, chopped
- 1 tablespoon tomato paste
- 1/4 teaspoon salt
- 1/4 teaspoon black pepper
- 1/2 pound turkey Italian sausage, casings removed
- Shredded mozzarella cheese

1. Combine tomatoes with juice, broth, mushrooms, onion, tomato paste, salt and pepper in **CROCK-POT®** slow cooker.

2. Shape sausage into marble-size balls. Gently stir into soup mixture. Cover; cook on LOW 6 to 7 hours. Serve with cheese.

Makes 4 servings

Pork Tenderloin with Cabbage

       3 cups shredded red cabbage
   $1/4$ cup chopped onion
   $1/4$ cup chicken broth or water
       1 clove garlic, minced
  $11/2$ pounds pork tenderloin
   $3/4$ cup apple juice concentrate
       3 tablespoons honey mustard
  $11/2$ tablespoons Worcestershire sauce

1. Place cabbage, onion, broth and garlic in **CROCK-POT®** slow cooker. Place pork over cabbage mixture. Combine apple juice concentrate, mustard and Worcestershire sauce in small bowl. Pour over pork.

2. Cover; cook on LOW 6 to 8 hours or on HIGH 3 to 4 hours. Slice pork and serve with cabbage and juices.

Makes 6 servings

Contents

Fun Finger Foods

Sweet Hot Chicken Wings

- 3 pounds chicken wings, tips removed and split at joints
- 6 tablespoons salsa
- 1/3 cup honey
- 2 1/2 tablespoons soy sauce
- 2 tablespoons Dijon mustard
- 1 tablespoon vegetable oil
- 1 1/2 teaspoons grated fresh ginger
- 1/4 teaspoon grated orange peel
- 1/4 teaspoon grated lemon peel
- Blue cheese dressing (optional)

1. Place wings in 13×9-inch baking dish. Combine salsa, honey, soy sauce, mustard, oil, ginger, orange peel and lemon peel in small bowl; mix well. Pour over wings. Cover; marinate in refrigerator at least 6 hours or overnight.

2. Preheat oven to 400°F. Place wings in single layer on foil-lined, 15×10-inch jelly-roll pan. Pour marinade evenly over wings. Bake 40 to 45 minutes until brown. Transfer as many wings to **CROCK-POT® LITTLE DIPPER®** slow cooker as will fit. Serve with blue cheese dressing.

Makes about 3 dozen servings

Mini Carnitas Tacos

> 1 1/2 pounds boneless pork loin, cut into 1-inch cubes
> 1 onion, finely chopped
> 1/2 cup chicken broth
> 1 tablespoon chili powder
> 2 teaspoons ground cumin
> 1 teaspoon dried oregano
> 1/2 teaspoon minced canned chipotle peppers in adobo sauce
> 1/2 cup pico de gallo
> 2 tablespoons chopped fresh cilantro
> 1/2 teaspoon salt
> 12 (6-inch) flour or corn tortillas
> 3/4 cup (about 3 ounces) shredded sharp Cheddar cheese (optional)
> 3 tablespoons sour cream (optional)

1. Combine pork, onion, broth, chili powder, cumin, oregano and chipotle peppers in **CROCK-POT®** slow cooker. Cover; cook on LOW 6 hours or on HIGH 3 hours or until pork is very tender. Pour off excess cooking liquid.

2. Shred pork with two forks; stir in pico de gallo, cilantro and salt. Cover and keep warm on LOW or WARM until serving.

3. Cut 3 circles from each tortilla with 2-inch biscuit cutter. Top each with pork and garnish with cheese and sour cream. Serve warm.

Makes 36 mini tacos

Soy-Braised Chicken Wings

- ¼ cup *each* dry sherry and soy sauce
- 3 tablespoons sugar
- 2 tablespoons cornstarch
- 2 tablespoons minced garlic, divided
- 2 teaspoons red pepper flakes
- 12 chicken wings (about 2½ pounds), tips removed and split at joints
- 2 tablespoons vegetable oil
- 3 green onions, cut into 1-inch pieces
- ¼ cup chicken broth
- 1 teaspoon sesame oil
- 1 tablespoon sesame seeds, toasted*

*To toast sesame seeds, place in small skillet. Shake skillet over medium-low heat 3 minutes or until seeds begin to pop and turn golden. Remove from heat.

1. Combine sherry, soy sauce, sugar, cornstarch, 1 tablespoon garlic and red pepper flakes in large bowl; mix well. Reserve ¼ cup marinade. Stir wings into remaining marinade. Cover; marinate in refrigerator 8 hours.

2. Drain wings; discard marinade. Heat oil in large skillet over high heat. Add wings in batches; cook 3 minutes or until browned. Remove to **CROCK-POT®** slow cooker. Add remaining 1 tablespoon garlic and green onions to skillet; cook and stir 30 seconds. Stir in broth; pour over wings.

3. Cover; cook on HIGH 2 hours. Add sesame oil to reserved marinade; mix well. Pour over wings; sprinkle with sesame seeds.

Makes about 2 dozen wings

Maple-Glazed Meatballs

- 1 1/2 cups ketchup
- 1 cup maple syrup
- 1/3 cup soy sauce
- 1 tablespoon quick-cooking tapioca
- 1 1/2 teaspoons ground allspice
- 1 teaspoon dry mustard
- 2 packages (about 16 ounces each) frozen fully cooked meatballs, partially thawed and separated
- 1 can (20 ounces) pineapple chunks in juice, drained

1. Combine ketchup, maple syrup, soy sauce, tapioca, allspice and mustard in **CROCK-POT®** slow cooker.

2. Carefully stir meatballs and pineapple chunks into ketchup mixture. Cover; cook on LOW 5 to 6 hours.

3. Stir before serving. Serve warm; insert cocktail picks, if desired.

Makes about 4 dozen meatballs

Tip: For a quick main dish, serve meatballs over hot cooked rice.

Creamy Duxelles Dip

- 1 package (10 ounces) cremini or "baby bella" mushrooms
- 1 tablespoon unsalted butter
- 2 tablespoons chopped shallots
- 2 cloves garlic, minced
- $1^1/_2$ teaspoons chopped fresh marjoram
- $1^1/_2$ tablespoons dry sherry
- $1/_8$ teaspoon salt
  Pinch black pepper
- $2^1/_2$ tablespoons crème fraîche
- $1/_2$ tablespoon grated Parmesan cheese
  Toasted baguette slices, flat bread or multi-grain crackers

1. Place mushrooms in food processor and pulse until finely chopped.

2. Melt butter in large nonstick skillet over medium-high heat. Add shallots and garlic; cook 4 to 5 minutes or until softened, stirring occasionally. Stir in mushrooms and marjoram. Cook 8 to 9 minutes or until all liquid has evaporated and the mushrooms begin to brown, stirring occasionally. Add sherry, salt and pepper; cook 1 minute.

3. Coat **CROCK-POT® LITTLE DIPPER®** slow cooker with nonstick cooking spray. Add mushroom mixture, crème fraîche and cheese. Cover; heat 1 hour. Stir well and serve with toasted baguette slices, flat bread or multi-grain crackers.

Makes about $1^1/_4$ cups

Variation: Try this dip served over steak or roast chicken.

Shrimp Fondue Dip

3 tablespoons butter, divided
8 ounces small raw shrimp, peeled
1 teaspoon seafood seasoning
$1/4$ teaspoon black pepper
$1/4$ teaspoon ground red pepper
1 tablespoon all-purpose flour
$3/4$ cup half-and-half
$3/8$ cup (about 3 ounces) shredded Gruyère cheese
$1/4$ cup dry white wine
1 teaspoon Dijon mustard
Sliced French bread

1. Melt 2 tablespoons butter in medium saucepan over medium heat. Add shrimp and sprinkle with seafood seasoning, black pepper and red pepper. Cook 3 minutes or until shrimp are opaque, stirring frequently. Transfer to medium bowl.

2. Melt remaining 1 tablespoon butter in same saucepan over medium heat. Stir in flour; cook and stir 2 minutes. Gradually stir in half-and-half. Cook and stir until mixture comes to a boil and thickens. Add cheese; cook and stir until cheese is melted. Stir in wine, mustard and cooked shrimp with any accumulated juices.

3. Coat **CROCK-POT® LITTLE DIPPER®** slow cooker with nonstick cooking spray. Fill with warm dip. Serve with sliced French bread.

Makes about 1³/₄ cups

Fun Finger Foods

Spicy Korean Chicken Wings

  2 tablespoons peanut oil, plus additional for frying
  2 tablespoons grated fresh ginger
  1/2 cup reduced-sodium soy sauce
  1/4 cup cider vinegar
  1/4 cup honey
  1/4 cup chili garlic sauce
  2 tablespoons orange juice
  1 tablespoon sesame oil
  18 chicken wings or drummettes
    Sesame seeds (optional)

1. Heat 2 tablespoons peanut oil in medium skillet over medium-high heat. Add ginger; cook and stir 2 minutes. Add soy sauce, vinegar, honey, chili garlic sauce, orange juice and sesame oil; cook and stir 2 minutes.

2. Heat 2 inches peanut oil in large heavy saucepan over medium-high heat until oil is 350°F to 375°F.

3. Rinse wings under cold water; pat dry with paper towels. Remove and discard wing tips. Add wings to peanut oil and cook about 8 to 10 minutes or until crispy and brown and chicken is cooked through. Remove wings from peanut oil; drain on paper towels.

4. Add wings to sauce; toss to coat. Fill **CROCK-POT® LITTLE DIPPER®** slow cooker with as many wings as will fit. Reserve and keep warm any extra wings, refilling **CROCK-POT® LITTLE DIPPER®** slow cooker as space allows. Sprinkle with sesame seeds, if desired.

Makes 6 to 8 servings

Bacon-Wrapped Fingerling Potatoes with Thyme

- 1 **pound fingerling potatoes**
- 2 **tablespoons olive oil**
- 1 **tablespoon minced fresh thyme**
- $1/2$ **teaspoon black pepper**
- $1/4$ **teaspoon paprika**
- $1/2$ **pound bacon**
- $1/4$ **cup chicken broth**

1. Toss potatoes with oil, thyme, pepper and paprika in large bowl.

2. Cut each bacon slice in half lengthwise; wrap half slice bacon tightly around each potato.

3. Heat large skillet over medium heat; add potatoes. Reduce heat to medium-low; cook until lightly browned and bacon has tightened around potatoes.

4. Place potatoes in **CROCK-POT®** slow cooker. Add broth. Cover; cook on HIGH 3 hours.

Makes 4 to 6 servings

Tip: This appetizer can be made even more eye-catching with rare varieties of potatoes. Many interesting types of small potatoes can be found at farmers' markets. Purple potatoes, about the size of fingerling potatoes, can add some more color and spunk to this dish.

Light Bites & Starters

Coconut Rice Pudding

- 2 cups water
- 1 cup uncooked converted long grain rice
- 1 tablespoon unsalted butter
- Pinch salt
- 2 1/4 cups evaporated milk
- 1 can (about 14 ounces) cream of coconut
- 1/2 cup golden raisins
- 3 egg yolks, beaten
- Grated peel of 2 limes
- 1 teaspoon vanilla
- Toasted shredded coconut (optional)

1. Place water, rice, butter and salt in medium saucepan. Bring to a boil over high heat, stirring frequently. Reduce heat to low. Cover; cook 10 to 12 minutes. Remove from heat. Let stand, covered, 5 minutes.

2. Meanwhile, add evaporated milk, cream of coconut, raisins, egg yolks, lime peel and vanilla to **CROCK-POT®** slow cooker; mix well. Add rice; stir until blended. Cover; cook on LOW 4 hours or on HIGH 2 hours, stirring every 30 minutes. Garnish with toasted coconut.

Makes 6 servings

Apple-Cranberry Crêpes

    1 large baking apple, such as Gala or Jonathan, peeled
      and cut into 6 wedges
    1 large tart apple, such as Granny Smith, peeled and cut
      into 6 wedges
 1/4 cup dried sweetened cranberries or cherries
    2 tablespoons lemon juice
 1/2 teaspoon plus 1/8 teaspoon ground cinnamon, divided
 1/8 teaspoon *each* ground nutmeg and ground cloves
    1 tablespoon butter
 1/4 cup orange juice
    1 tablespoon sugar
 3/4 teaspoon cornstarch
 1/4 teaspoon almond extract
    4 prepared crêpes
    1 cup vanilla ice cream (optional)

1. Coat **CROCK-POT®** slow cooker with nonstick cooking spray.
Place apple wedges, cranberries, lemon juice, ½ teaspoon cinnamon,
nutmeg and cloves in **CROCK-POT®** slow cooker; toss to coat. Cover;
cook on LOW 2 hours. Stir butter into apple mixture just until melted.

2. Combine orange juice, sugar, cornstarch and almond extract in
small bowl; stir until cornstarch dissolves. Stir into apple mixture; mix
well. Turn **CROCK-POT®** slow cooker to HIGH; cover; cook on HIGH
15 minutes to thicken sauce slightly.

3. Spoon apple mixture evenly down center of each crêpe. Fold
edges over; place crêpes, seam sides down, on plates. Sprinkle with
remaining ⅛ teaspoon cinnamon. Serve with ice cream, if desired.

Makes 4 servings

Saag Paneer

- 2 onions, finely chopped
- 8 cloves garlic, minced
- 1 teaspoon ground coriander
- 1 teaspoon ground cumin
- $1/2$ teaspoon pumpkin pie spice
- $1/2$ teaspoon cardamom
- $1/2$ teaspoon salt
- 2 packages (10 ounces each) frozen chopped spinach, thawed and squeezed dry
- 2 packages (9 ounces each) frozen chopped creamed spinach, thawed
- 2 tablespoons butter
- 8 ounces paneer or firm tofu, cut into $1/2$-inch cubes

1. Combine onions, garlic, coriander, cumin, pumpkin pie spice, cardamom and salt in **CROCK-POT®** slow cooker. Add spinach, creamed spinach and butter. Cover; cook on LOW 4½ to 5 hours or until onions are soft.

2. Add paneer; cover and cook on LOW 30 minutes or until paneer is heated through.

Makes 10 servings

Spring Pea and Mint Broth Soup

   8 **cups water**
   3 **carrots, cut into chunks**
   2 **onions, coarsely chopped**
   2 to 3 **leeks, coarsely chopped**
   2 **stalks celery, cut into chunks**
   1 **bunch fresh mint**
   3 to 4 **cups fresh spring peas or 1 bag (32 ounces) frozen peas**
   1 **tablespoon fresh lemon juice**
      Kosher salt and black pepper
      Creme fraîche or sour cream

1. Combine water, carrots, onions, leeks, celery and mint in **CROCK-POT®** slow cooker. Cover; cook on HIGH 5 hours.

2. Add peas and lemon juice. Cover; cook on LOW 4 to 5 hours or on HIGH 2 to 3 hours. Season with salt and pepper. Ladle soup into bowls and garnish with dollop of creme fraîche.

Makes 6 to 8 servings

Note: Whether using farmstand-fresh spring peas or frozen sweet peas, this soup is fun to make. The aroma of fresh mint that fills the house is reason enough to try it.

Scallop and Corn Chowder

        6 tablespoons butter, divided
        1 bunch leeks, cleaned well and diced
      3/4 pound pancetta, diced
        5 Yukon Gold potatoes, diced
    5 1/4 cups fish stock
        2 cups corn
        1 tablespoon minced fresh thyme, plus additional
          for garnish
      1/4 cup all-purpose flour
        1 pound sea scallops, quartered
        1 pint whipping cream
          Black pepper (optional)

1. Heat 2 tablespoons butter in skillet over medium-high heat. Add leeks; cook and stir until softened and just beginning to brown. Transfer to **CROCK-POT®** slow cooker.

2. Cook pancetta until lightly browned in same skillet over medium heat; transfer to **CROCK-POT®** slow cooker. Add potatoes, stock, corn and 1 tablespoon thyme. Cover; cook on LOW 4 to 6 hours or on HIGH 2 to 3 hours or until potatoes are tender.

3. Combine remaining 4 tablespoons butter and flour in large saucepan over medium heat. Cook and stir to make a thick, golden brown paste. Stir in 1 cup cooking liquid from **CROCK-POT®** slow cooker. Stir until well blended and return mixture to **CROCK-POT®** slow cooker. Add scallops; cook 10 minutes or until just cooked through. Stir in cream. Garnish with pepper and additional thyme.

Makes 6 to 8 servings

Pesto Rice and Beans

      1 can (about 15 ounces) Great Northern beans,
         rinsed and drained
      1 can (about 14 ounces) chicken broth
    3/4 cup uncooked converted long grain rice
  1 1/2 cups frozen cut green beans, thawed and drained
    1/2 cup prepared pesto
         Grated Parmesan cheese (optional)

1. Combine Great Northern beans, broth and rice in **CROCK-POT®** slow cooker. Cover; cook on LOW 2 hours.

2. Stir in green beans. Cover; cook on LOW 1 hour or until rice and beans are tender.

3. Remove stoneware to heatproof surface. Stir in pesto and cheese, if desired. Cover; let stand 5 minutes or until cheese is melted. Serve immediately.

Makes 8 servings

Tip: Choose converted long grain rice (or Arborio rice when suggested) or wild rice for best results. Long, slow cooking can turn other types of rice into mush; if you prefer to use another type of rice instead of converted rice, cook it on the stove-top and add it to the **CROCK-POT®** slow cooker during the last 15 minutes of cooking.

Raspberry-Balsamic Glazed Meatballs

- 1 **bag (2 pounds) frozen fully cooked meatballs**
- 1 **cup raspberry preserves**
- 3 **tablespoons sugar**
- 3 **tablespoons balsamic vinegar**
- 1 **tablespoon plus 1 1/2 teaspoons Worcestershire sauce**
- 1/4 **teaspoon red pepper flakes**
- 1 **tablespoon grated fresh ginger (optional)**

1. Coat **CROCK-POT®** slow cooker with nonstick cooking spray. Add frozen meatballs; set aside.

2. Combine preserves, sugar, vinegar, Worcestershire sauce and red pepper flakes in small microwavable bowl. Microwave on HIGH 45 seconds; stir. Microwave 15 seconds or until melted (mixture will be chunky). Reserve ½ cup mixture. Pour remaining mixture over meatballs; toss to coat well. Cover; cook on LOW 5 hours or on HIGH 2½ hours.

3. Turn **CROCK-POT®** slow cooker to HIGH. Stir in ginger, if desired, and reserved ½ cup preserve mixture. Cook, uncovered, on HIGH 15 to 20 minutes or until thickened slightly, stirring occasionally.

Makes about **16** *servings*

Easiest Three-Cheese Fondue

     2 cups (8 ounces) shredded mild or sharp Cheddar cheese
   3/4 cup reduced-fat (2%) milk
   1/2 cup crumbled blue cheese
     1 package (3 ounces) cream cheese, cut into cubes
   1/4 cup finely chopped onion
     1 tablespoon all-purpose flour
     1 tablespoon butter or margarine
     2 cloves garlic, minced
     4 to 6 drops hot pepper sauce
   1/8 teaspoon ground red pepper
       Breadsticks and assorted fresh vegetables for dipping

1. Combine all ingredients except breadsticks and vegetables in **CROCK-POT®** slow cooker. Cover; cook on LOW 2 to 2½ hours, stirring once or twice, until cheeses are melted and smooth.

2. Turn **CROCK-POT®** slow cooker to HIGH. Cook on HIGH 1 to 1½ hours or until heated through. Serve with breadsticks and fresh vegetables for dipping.

Makes 8 servings

Tip: To reduce the total fat in this recipe, replace the Cheddar cheese and cream cheese with reduced-fat Cheddar and cream cheeses.

Tailgating

Cranberry-Barbecue Chicken Wings

    3 pounds chicken wings, tips removed and split at joints
      Salt and black pepper
    1 jar (12 ounces) cranberry-orange relish
  1/2 cup barbecue sauce
    2 tablespoons quick-cooking tapioca
    1 tablespoon prepared mustard
      Orange slices (optional)

1. Preheat broiler. Place wings on rack in broiler pan; season with salt and pepper. Broil 4 to 5 inches from heat for 10 to 12 minutes or until browned, turning once. Transfer wings to **CROCK-POT®** slow cooker.

2. Combine relish, barbecue sauce, tapioca and mustard in small bowl. Pour over wings. Cover; cook on LOW 4 to 5 hours. Serve with orange slices, if desired.

Makes about 16 appetizer servings

Mexican Cheese Soup

1 pound pasteurized process cheese product, cubed
1 pound ground beef, cooked and drained
1 can (about 15 ounces) kidney beans, undrained
1 can (about 14 ounces) diced tomatoes with green chiles, undrained
1 can (about 14 ounces) stewed tomatoes, undrained
1 can (8³/₄ ounces) corn, undrained
1 envelope taco seasoning
1 jalapeño pepper, diced* (optional)
  Corn chips (optional)

Jalapeño peppers can sting and irritate the skin, so wear rubber gloves when handling peppers and do not touch your eyes.

1. Coat **CROCK-POT®** slow cooker with nonstick cooking spray. Add cheese, beef, beans, tomatoes with chiles, stewed tomatoes with juice, corn, taco seasoning and jalapeño pepper, if desired. Mix well.

2. Cover; cook on LOW 4 to 5 hours or on HIGH 3 hours. Serve with corn chips, if desired.

Makes 6 to 8 servings

Brats in Beer

1¹/₂ pounds bratwurst (about 5 or 6 links)
   1 bottle (12 ounces) amber ale or beer
   1 onion, thinly sliced
   2 tablespoons packed light brown sugar
   2 tablespoons red wine or cider vinegar
     Spicy brown mustard
     Cocktail rye bread

1. Combine bratwurst, ale, onion, brown sugar and vinegar in **CROCK-POT®** slow cooker. Cover; cook on LOW 4 to 5 hours.

2. Remove bratwurst from cooking liquid. Cut into ½-inch-thick slices.

3. Spread mustard on cocktail rye bread. Top with bratwurst slices and onion. (Whole brats also can be served on toasted split French or Italian rolls.)

Makes 30 to 36 appetizers

Tip: Choose a light-tasting beer when cooking brats. Hearty ales can leave the meat tasting slightly bitter.

Tropical Chicken Wings

    1 jar (12 ounces) pineapple preserves
$1/2$ cup soy sauce
$1/2$ cup chopped green onions
    3 tablespoons fresh lime juice
    2 tablespoons honey
    1 tablespoon minced garlic
    2 teaspoons sriracha sauce*
$1/4$ teaspoon ground allspice
    3 pounds chicken wings, tips removed and split at joints
    1 tablespoon toasted sesame seeds

Sriracha is a spicy chile sauce made from dried chiles and used as a condiment in several Asian cuisines. It can be found in the ethnic section of major supermarkets, but an equal amount of hot pepper sauce may be substituted.

1. Combine all ingredients except wings and sesame seeds in **CROCK-POT®** slow cooker; stir well.

2. Add wings to sauce and stir to coat. Cover; cook on LOW 3 to 4 hours or until wings are fork-tender.

3. Sprinkle with sesame seeds just before serving.

Makes 6 to 8 servings

Parmesan Potato Wedges

  2   pounds red potatoes, cut into $1/2$-inch wedges
$1/4$ cup finely chopped yellow onion
$1^1/2$ teaspoons dried oregano
$1/2$ teaspoon salt
$1/4$ teaspoon black pepper, or to taste
  2   tablespoons butter, cut into small pieces
$1/4$ cup grated Parmesan cheese

Layer potatoes, onion, oregano, salt, pepper and butter in **CROCK-POT®** slow cooker. Cover; cook on HIGH 4 hours. Transfer potatoes to serving platter and sprinkle with cheese.

Makes 6 servings

Moroccan Spiced Chicken Wings

1/4 cup orange juice

3 tablespoons tomato paste

2 teaspoons ground cumin

1 teaspoon curry powder

1 teaspoon ground turmeric

1/2 teaspoon ground cinnamon

1/2 teaspoon ground ginger

1 teaspoon salt

1 tablespoon olive oil

5 pounds chicken wings, tips removed and split at joints

1. Whisk orange juice, tomato paste, cumin, curry powder, turmeric, cinnamon, ginger and salt in large bowl; set aside.

2. Heat oil in large nonstick skillet over medium-high heat. Add wings and brown in several batches, about 6 minutes per batch. Transfer wings to bowl with sauce as they are cooked. Toss well to coat.

3. Place wings in **CROCK-POT®** slow cooker. Cover; cook on LOW 6 to 7 hours or on HIGH 3 to 3½ hours or until tender.

Makes 8 servings

Recipe Index

Recipe Index

Recipe Index